The SHOWIEST Animals Around

Written by Charis Mather

©2026
BookLife Publishing Ltd.
King's Lynn, Norfolk
PE30 2HN, UK

All rights reserved.
Printed in the UK.

A catalogue record for this book is available from the British Library.

HB ISBN: 978-1-80505-741-3
PB ISBN: 978-1-80505-957-8

Written by:
Charis Mather

Edited by:
Rebecca Phillips-Bartlett

Designed by:
Amelia Harris

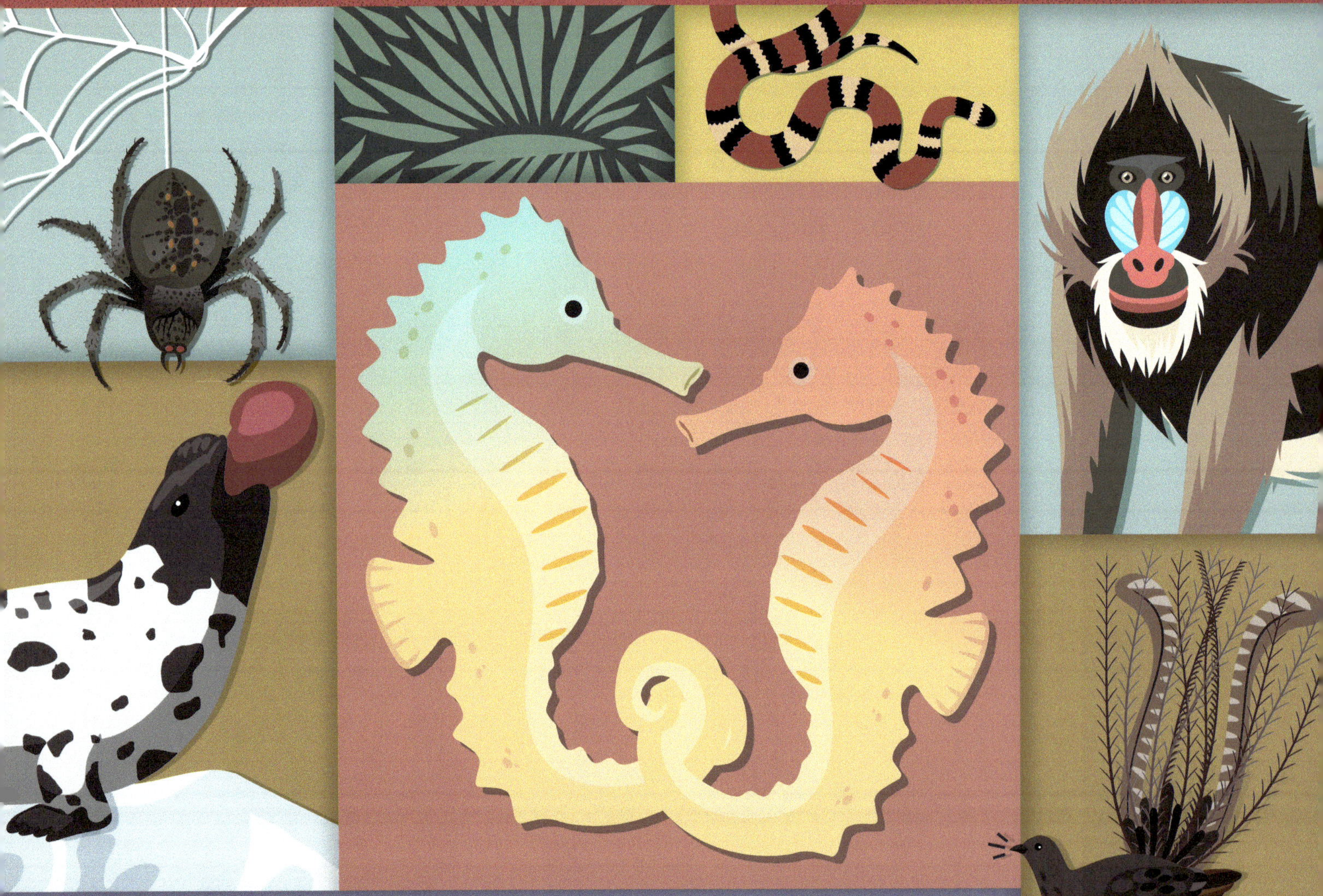

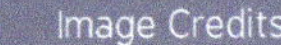

Image Credits

Images courtesy of Shutterstock.com, unless otherwise stated.

Cover and Recurring – sweet kiwi, hazecats, Lifestyle Graphic, Quang Vinh Tran, Harashchuk Oksana, Olga_Serova, Robusta, ace03, Alfmaler. 4–5 – Sourabh Bharti, MikhailPopov, janista, ALEXEY GRIGOREV, Amanita Silvicora, SaveJungle, Kelp Creative, Cyudeshbuhu, YummyBuum, Quang Vinh Tran. 6–7 – Itz Chinmoy. 8–9 – Captain_Dnl, Arunee Rodloy, sproba, Net Vector, Jan Bures. 10–11 – DWI YULIANTO, 111Nataliia111, Krishna Sekhar, Shawn Hempel, Maquiladora, Andrei Zhukov, Val_Iva, U-Design, Evgeniia Mokeeva. 12–13 – Macrovector, Zaie, Maquiladora, klyaksun, the8monkey. 14–15 – Simon Mustoe, Avisnana, Quang Vinh Tran, baby corn, HappyPictures, Richard Seeley, Simon Mustoe, Alaskan Wildlife. 16–17 – Pavaphon Supanantananont, Maquiladora, StockSmartStart, YummyBuum, Sabelskaya, Volha Valadzionak, Quang Vinh Tran, Berendje Fotografie. 18–19 – Paper Trident, Melissa Burovac, Maquiladora, FoxGrafy, GoodStudio, quinky, Trigubova Irina, Ihsan Faraby ST. 20–21 – Simon Dannhauer, Louise Cole, Aratehortua, zunaki, hana honoka.

CONTENTS

Words that look like this can be found in the glossary on page 24.

BEING AN ANIMAL IS HARD WORK

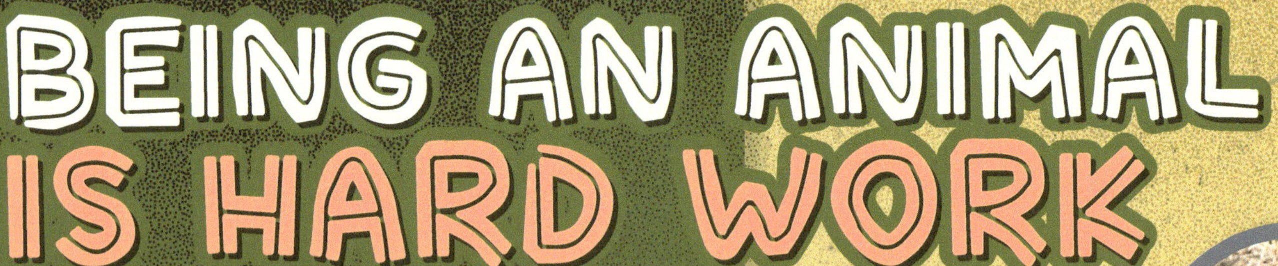

It's not easy being an animal. From the incy-winciest insect to the most powerful predator, all animals have to work hard to get what they want.

But what *do* animals want? It's simple, really. They want to survive, and they want to thrive!

In other words, animals want…

For many animals, how well they can survive
comes down to who has the **showiest** . . .

looks,

moves,

or **skills.**

Which animals have the most
wow-worthy way of showing off?
That's up to you to decide!

COLOURFUL COMMUNICATION

Sending an unmissable message

Poison dart frogs speak with their skin. Their bright colours scream "Don't eat me . . . or else!" Any animal looking for a little snack would be wise to take this warning seriously!

Poison dart frogs get their toxicity from the poisonous insects they eat.

This frog's poison is strong enough to kill 20,000 mice.

Pretending to be poisonous

Milk snakes copy the bright colours of <u>venomous</u> coral snakes. It's a clever way to keep predators from pestering them.

Blue in the cheeks

Male mandrills use their bare red and blue faces and backsides to win respect from other animals. Female mandrills love these flashy features.

FRESH FITS

Some animals get more than one outfit to show off in.

Nature's mood ring
Chameleons change colour based on how they are feeling.
Things that affect a chameleon's colour include . . .

Old age

Feeling too hot

Feeling sick

Feeling excited

Feeling scared

Looking for a fight!

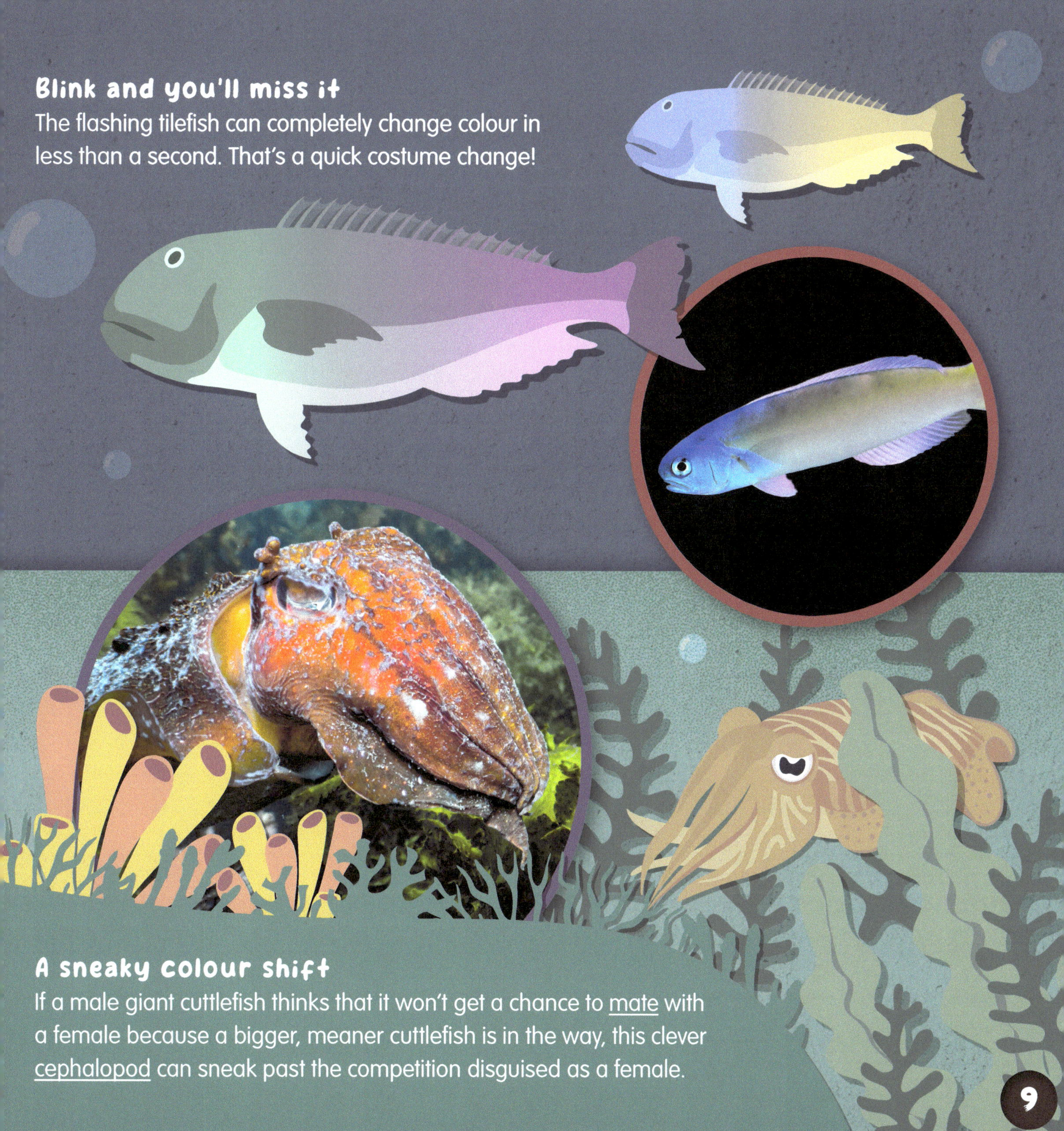

Blink and you'll miss it

The flashing tilefish can completely change colour in less than a second. That's a quick costume change!

A sneaky colour shift

If a male giant cuttlefish thinks that it won't get a chance to <u>mate</u> with a female because a bigger, meaner cuttlefish is in the way, this clever <u>cephalopod</u> can sneak past the competition disguised as a female.

FANCY FASHION

Looking good isn't all about colour. Some animals have fabulous features to flaunt.

A fan-tastic tail

Male peacocks flutter their fan of <u>iridescent</u> tail feathers to impress females with the flashing colours and rattling sounds. Their longest feathers are about 150 centimetres long—longer than their actual bodies!

Thrilling frills

Frilled dragons can't breathe fire, but they can puff out an impressive fiery-coloured neck ruff.

Puffed up and ready for a party

There is no need for balloons when hooded seals are at the party. The males blow their own balloons, straight out of their noses, as a way to show off. These balloons are called nasal sacks.

GLOWING OFF

Even darkness can't take the spotlight away from these animals.

Hanging glow
Glowworms hang out in dark caves—literally!

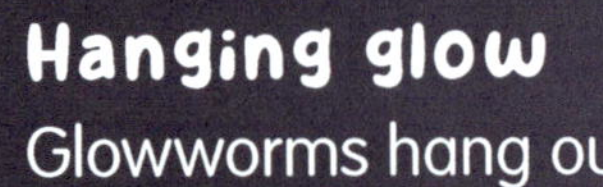

Fly and flash
Some fireflies time their glows so that their flashing matches up with other fireflies.

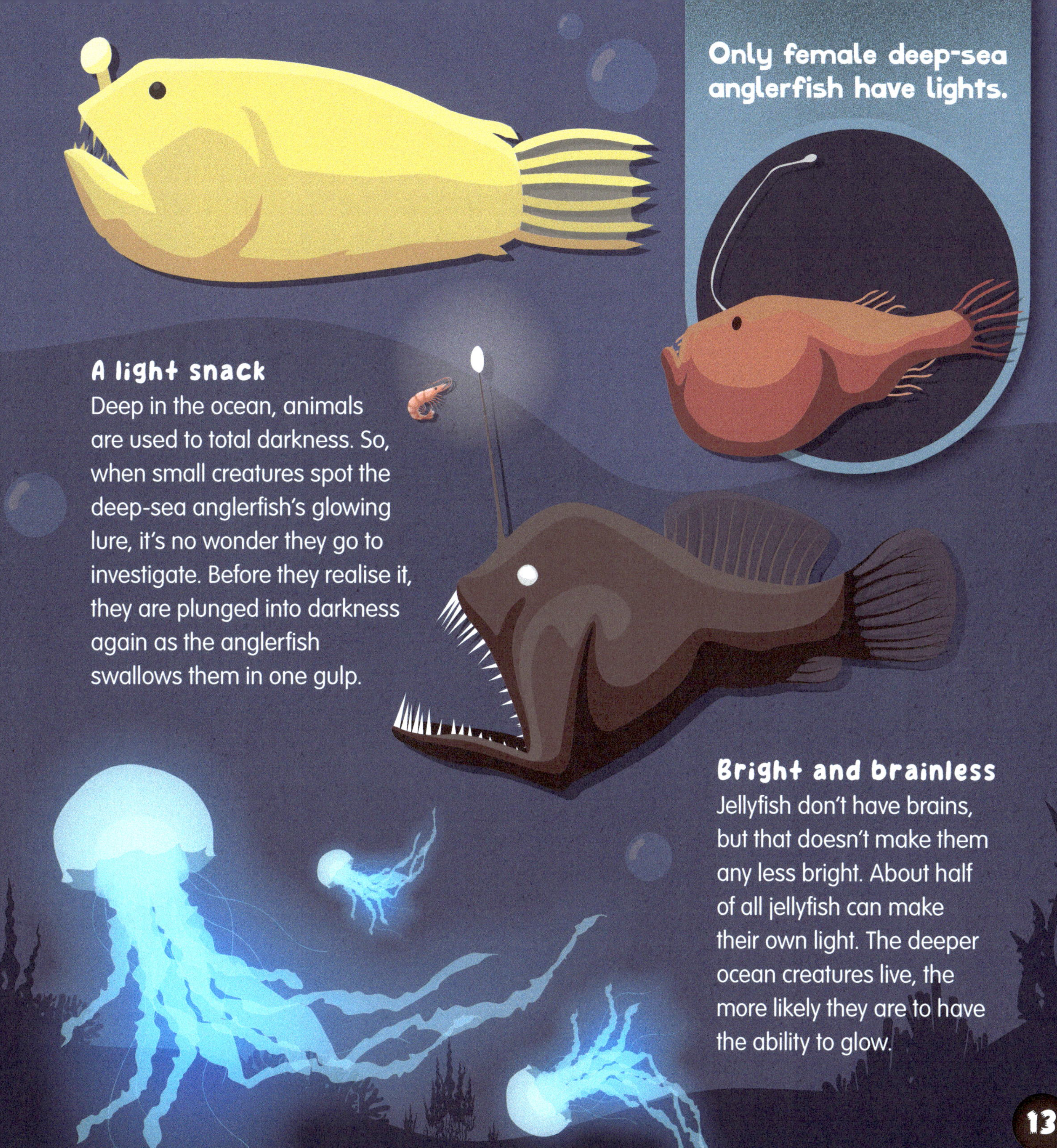

A light snack

Deep in the ocean, animals are used to total darkness. So, when small creatures spot the deep-sea anglerfish's glowing lure, it's no wonder they go to investigate. Before they realise it, they are plunged into darkness again as the anglerfish swallows them in one gulp.

Bright and brainless

Jellyfish don't have brains, but that doesn't make them any less bright. About half of all jellyfish can make their own light. The deeper ocean creatures live, the more likely they are to have the ability to glow.

MAKING MOVES

Dance or die

For some wildlife, good dance moves are a must.

Male peacock spiders put everything into their mating dance. Expect to see such dance moves as . . .

- Robot arms
- The side-to-side shuffle
- The backside bop
- The fluttering fan
- Spinning in circles

If the female isn't impressed, she will eat the disappointing dancer!

Seahorses show their love by dancing together every morning. Their dances can last up to nine hours.

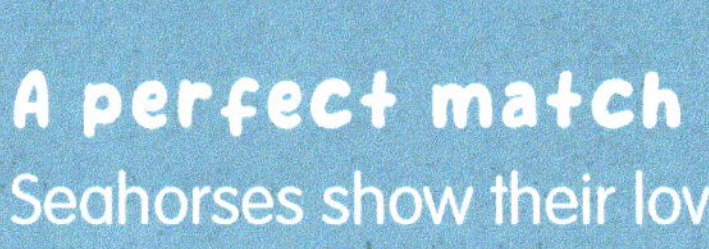

Fluttering hearts

Hummingbirds are the only birds that can fly backwards, upside down and hover in place.

Stunning stunts

Stoats sometimes stun their prey by spinning, jumping and doing other strange stunts in front of them.

LOUD AND CLEAR

A wild wake-up call

Howler monkeys have a special shell-like <u>organ</u> in their throat that makes their howls extra loud. The raspy roars from a group of howler monkeys can be heard from nearly five kilometres away.

Copycat? Copybird!

Lyrebirds can copy the calls of other birds, as well as car alarms, camera clicks and human speech!

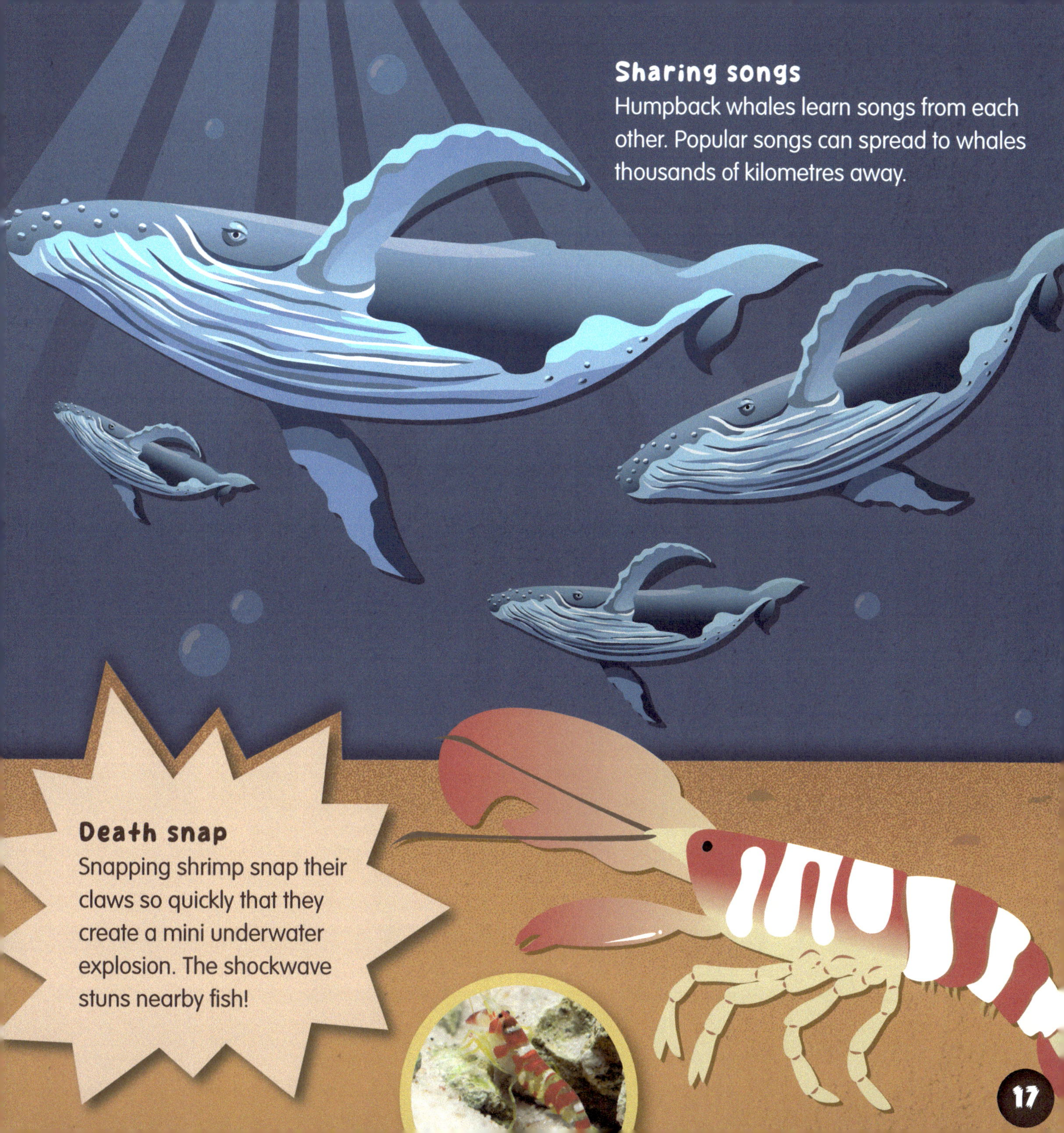

Sharing songs

Humpback whales learn songs from each other. Popular songs can spread to whales thousands of kilometres away.

Death snap

Snapping shrimp snap their claws so quickly that they create a mini underwater explosion. The shockwave stuns nearby fish!

MAY THE BEST BUILDER WIN

Some animals show off their skills by building structures that stand out.

Underwater art

Male pufferfish wriggle through the sand on the sea floor, creating pretty patterns with their bodies. These circles of sand are perfect for female pufferfish to use as nests.

This is what pufferfish look like when they aren't puffed up.

Exterior decorators

Bowerbirds build stick structures called bowers.
They decorate them using flowers, feathers,
berries, shells, stones and
whatever else they
can find.

Basket weavers

Weaver birds have a special skill
that no other bird has—they can tie
knots! They use this skill to build their
hanging homes out of woven grass.

WHIFFY WILDLIFE

Nothing gets someone's attention quite like a stinky smell.

Stink-Off

When male lemurs fall out, they have a stink-off. They cover their long tails with a stinky smell from their scent <u>glands</u>. Then they wave their smelly tails at each other until one of them can't bear the stench any longer. The lemur who backs off first loses.

Washing with wee

Male capuchin monkeys don't wash with soap and water like humans do. They scrub their bodies with their own wee!

Race to mate

If a female emperor moth is looking for a mate, she releases a scented message into the air. The males race to find the source of the smell.

ANIMALS WILL DO ANYTHING FOR ATTENTION

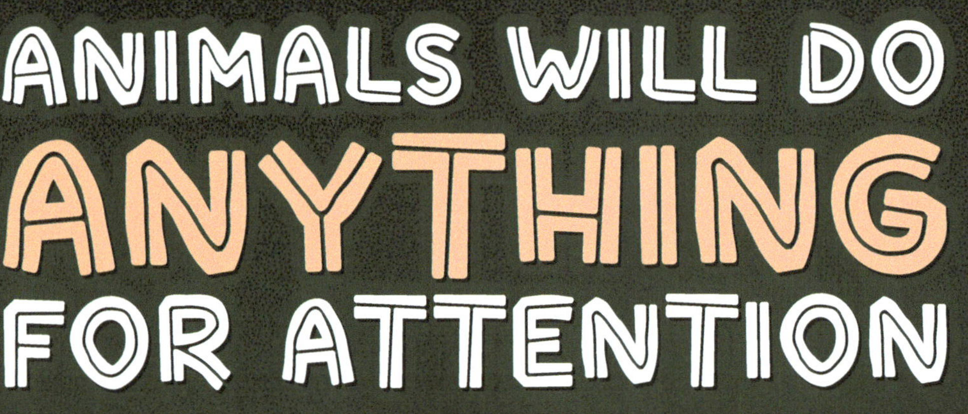

Colour changes

Glowing in the dark

Bright colours

Which animal gets the prize for being the showiest animal of them all?

Impressive body parts

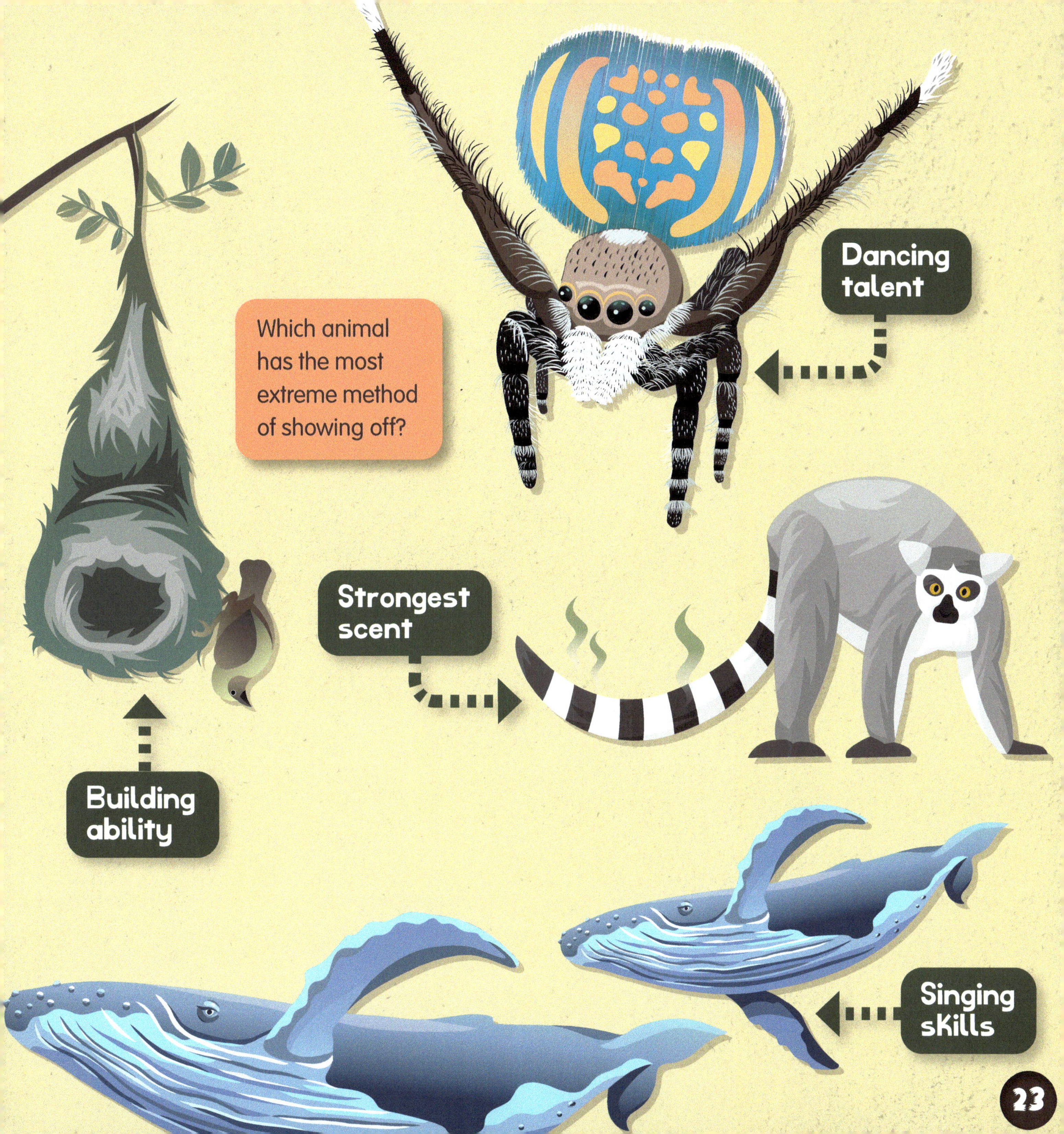

Which animal has the most extreme method of showing off?
Dancing talent
Strongest scent
Building ability
Singing skills
23

GLOSSARY

cephalopod animals from the group that contains octopuses and squids

glands parts of the body that produce chemicals

iridescent shimmering with colours that seem to change when seen from a different angle

mate to produce young with an animal of the same species

organ a part of a living thing that has a specific, important function

venomous able to poison another animal through a bite or a scratch

INDEX